W9-BMF-720

MACHINES ★ AT WORK

POLICE CARS

BY CYNTHIA ROBERTS

THE CHILD'S WORLD® • MANKATO, MINNESOTA

The Child's World®

Published in the United States of America by The Child's World®
1980 Lookout Drive • Mankato, MN 56003-1705
800-599-READ • www.childsworld.com

PHOTO CREDITS
© iStockphoto.com/Andrei Tchernov: 3
All other photos © David M. Budd Photography.

ACKNOWLEDGMENTS
The Child's World®: Mary Berendes, Publishing Director;
Katherine Stevenson, Editor

The Design Lab: Kathleen Petelinsek, Design and Page Production

LIBRARY OF CONGRESS CATALOGING-IN-PUBLICATION DATA
Roberts, Cynthia, 1960–
  Police cars / By Cynthia Roberts.
     p. cm. — (Machines at work)
  Includes bibliographical references and index.
  ISBN 1-59296-834-1 (lib. bdg. : alk. paper)
  1. Police vehicles—Juvenile literature. I. Title. II. Series.
  HV7936.V4R63 2007
  629.222088'3632—dc22   2006023299

5399141

⭐ Contents

Police cars are kept very clean.

⭐ What are police cars?

Police cars are **vehicles** driven by police officers. They help the officers do their jobs. They carry everything the officers need. They take the officers where they need to go—quickly!

⭐ What do police cars look like?

Police cars look like other cars. But they are different, too. Many police cars have special paint or markings. They have bright lights on top.

This police officer is starting work for the day. She works in Boulder, Colorado.

Police cars must be able to travel quickly during emergencies.

In **emergencies**, the bright lights flash and blink. Police cars have loud **sirens**, too. The lights and sirens let other drivers know the police car is coming.

Some police cars have no special paint or markings. Their bright lights and sirens are hidden. These **unmarked** cars look just like other people's cars. They are useful for some kinds of police work. In an emergency, the officer brings out the flashing light.

This unmarked car does not look like a police car!
The light goes on top only in emergencies.

Officers in police cars watch many things. They look at other cars. They watch people walking by. ⭐

★ Why do police officers need special cars?

Most police officers do a lot of driving. They need cars that are safe and do not break down. They need cars that can go fast. They need cars that can carry people who have broken the law. They need ways to stay in touch with other officers.

13

⭐ How do police cars work?

Police cars work just like other people's cars. An **engine** makes power that turns the wheels. The engine runs on gasoline. The driver uses a steering wheel to turn the car.

Driving a police car is like driving any other car.

Officers use their computers when the car is stopped. They often use their radios and telephones when the car is moving.

★ What is inside a police car?

Police officers use their car as an office. Today, police cars have computers. They have radios and telephones. Officers use these to talk to each other. They use them to find out what they need to know. Many police cars also have cameras.

17

Most police cars have a **barrier** between the front and back seats. People who have broken the law ride in the back seat. The barrier helps protect the officers.

18

The barrier has a clear window. The officers can see through the barrier to the back seat.

The officer in this car has stopped a person for speeding.

⍟ Are police cars important?

Police officers have very important jobs. They keep people safe. They need to get to emergencies quickly. Police cars help them do their jobs and stay safe. Police cars save lives every day!

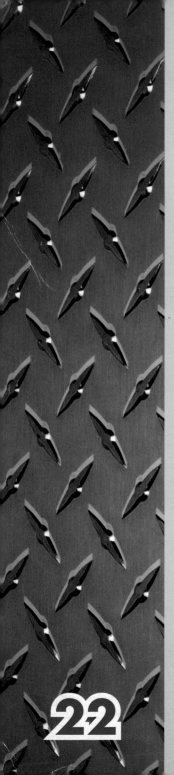

⭐ Glossary

barrier (BER-ree-ur) A barrier is something that blocks someone's way.

emergencies (ih-MUR-junt-seez) Emergencies are times of danger, when people must act quickly.

engine (EN-jun) An engine is a machine that makes something move.

sirens (SY-runz) Sirens make loud noises to let people know there is danger.

unmarked (un-MARKT) Something that is unmarked has no special colors or writing on it.

vehicles (VEE-uh-kullz) Vehicles are things that carry people or goods.

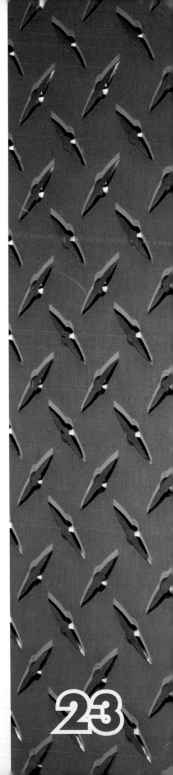

 Books

Auerbach, Annie, Jesus Redondo (illustrator), and Ican & Moxo (illustrators). *Police on Patrol.* New York: Little Simon, 2003.

McGuire, Leslie, and Joseph Mathieu (illustrator). *Big Mike's Police Car.* New York: Random House, 2003.

 Web Sites

Visit our Web site for lots of links about police cars:
http://www.childsworld.com/links
Note to parents, teachers, and librarians: We routinely check our Web links to make sure they're safe, active sites—so encourage your readers to check them out!

23

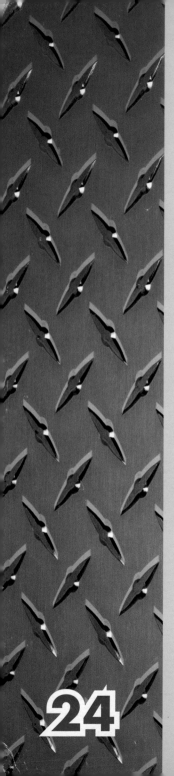

⭐ Index

⭐ About the Author

Even as a child, Cynthia Roberts knew she wanted to be a writer. She is always working to involve kids in reading and writing, and she loves spending time in the children's section of the library or bookstore. Cynthia enjoys gardening, traveling, and having fun with friends and family.